Published by Suzanne Elizabeth Kidd

Designed by DK Architects (Studio 4, Batley)
www.dkarchitects.net

Visit us at
www.quran4kids.co.uk

For the past seven years I have worked as a primary school teacher in a Muslim school, I am currently working as a Special Educational Needs teacher. Through my teaching degree, attending further training courses and work experience, I have gained great insight into how children learn. It is known that children learn in different ways, this book addresses the different teaching and learning styles, allowing children to be taught how to read the Quran in the most effective way.

After passing my Tajweed exam with The Jordanian Institute 'The Society of the Conservation of the Quran' it has made it possible for me to teach children Tajweed. As a parent and teacher I struggled to find a book which catered for children effectively, because of this experience I have written these books. My aim is to make learning Tajweed easy and fun for children. This book offers parents and teachers access to the appropriate resources and learning tools.

The books have been approved by the head of Al Manhal, a UK based organization which teaches Tajweed. Al Manhal is linked to 'The Society of the Conservation of Quran' in Jordan. The books have been used to teach pupils at two Islamic institutes, Manchester Muslim Prep School and Al Huda Zawiayh centre in Yorkshire. The books have also been used for home tutoring purposes and to teach children who have special educational needs. In all cases the books have been very successful in all aspects of children's learning.

This book is a step by step guide for parents and teachers to follow which makes Tajweed easy and fun for children to learn. There are clear objectives and teaching steps for each rule that is taught. After each lesson there are corresponding worksheets for the pupils to complete in their book and corresponding audio support on the website.

LEARNING STYLES

TEACHING STEPS

There are four main learning styles that children need to access to enable them to learn in the most effective way:

1. Kinaesthetic Learners - learn through practical experiences and taking an active role.

2. Auditory Learners - learn through hearing and listening to the concept being taught.

3. Visual Learners - learn through images, coloured pictures, diagrams and other visual aids.

4. Intellectual/Logical Learners - learn through analysing and thinking about the information being taught.

The Teacher's Guide has a series of very useful and clear teaching steps to follow. The following five steps ensure that pupils have an opportunity to learn in different ways e.g. through practical and visual activities alongside reading and writing activities. The same five steps are used on every page. There is also an extra 'Teaching Tip' at the bottom of some pages. An example of the five teaching steps is given below.

1) The pupils will be taught a letter or rule using visual flash cards, (this caters for the visual and auditory learner.)

2) The pupils will take part in a short activity to consolidate what has been taught in step 1 (this caters for the kinaesthetic learner.)

3) The pupils will write examples on a white board.

4) The pupils will listen to the pronunciation on the website, (this again caters for the auditory, visual and intellectual learner.)

5) The pupils will complete some worksheets after each lesson, (this caters for the visual, kinaesthetic and intellectual learners.)

There is also fun and helpful teaching ideas at the end of every lesson!

Lessons and Objectives

At the beginning of each lesson there will be some clear learning objectives. The objectives need to be stated to the pupil at the start of each session so they are clear about what it is they are going to learn. It also clarifies in the teacher's mind exactly what needs to be taught. Check at the end of the lesson if he/she feels they have achieved the learning objective. Not all of the teaching steps need to be taught every lesson, if the pupil is confident and only needs a short time spent on some of the rules, just pick and choose from the five steps and move on to the next lesson. If there is a lot of information covered in one lesson spread the lesson out over a few days or weeks.

Lesson Plan

There is a template Lesson plan at the back of the book which can be photocopied and used by teachers to help them plan and prepare for each lesson.

Assessment Sheets

There are some assessment sheets for teachers to use. Each assessment should be carried out at the end of the chapter to ensure the pupils have understood what has been taught before moving on to the next chapter. A brief explanation of how to use the assessments is given in the appropriate section.

Pupil's Work Sheets

The Pupils have their own work book, the lessons and worksheets correspond with each other. Alternatively the worksheets can be photocopied and handed out to each pupil as the lessons progress.

Website

The following website provides audio support and visual aids for the pupils to listen to after each lesson.

www.quran4kids.co.uk

CONTENTS

Chapter One teaches the articulation point of each letter, otherwise known as Makhaarij-Al-Huroof. The articulation point of each letter needs to be taught so each letter can be pronounced correctly. Different letters are pronounced from different parts of the throat, mouth and lips. The diagrams in this chapter show where each letter is pronounced from.

Teaching the alphabet starts in chapter Two. The letters are taught in the order of the alphabet however for the teacher's knowledge the letters have been grouped according to where they are pronounced from. There are no lessons or worksheets for this Chapter as it is for the teacher only and will be taught to the pupils in Chapter 2.

The letters have been divided into the following five groups.

1. The Throat - has three articulation points for six different letters which are pronounced from the bottom, middle, and top part of the throat.

2. The Lips - The lips have two articulation points for four letters.

3. The Tongue - It has ten articulation points for eighteen letters, they are divided into tip letters and non tip letters. The movement of the tongue is illustrated on the diagrams.

4. The empty space in the mouth and throat - this is the articulation point for the three lengthened letters, which are:

> Dammah followed by Wow Saakin,
> Kasrah followed by Yaa Saakin and
> Fat-hah followed by Alif Saakin

5) The nasal passage - From the nose towards the inside of the mouth, there is one articulation point, that of the Ghunnah sound.

Throat Letters

Letters pronounced from the throat
ء ﻫ ع ح خ غ

The letters Hamza and Haa are pronounced from the bottom part of the throat. Ein and Haa are pronounced from the middle part of the throat. Ghayn and Khaa are pronounced from the top part of the throat. The letters Ghayn and Khaa are heavy and the back part of the tongue should be elevated when pronouncing them. This is illustrated on the diagram.

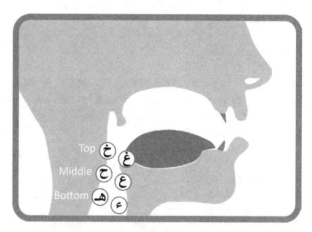

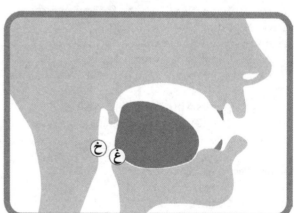

Lips

Letters pronounced from the lips

ب م و ف

Baa and Meem

Baa is pronounced between closed lips which then open. Meem is pronounced between closed lips with the nasal cavity open because it has the quality of Ghunna (a nasal sound emitted from the nasal passage.) This illustrated by the arrows on the diagram below.

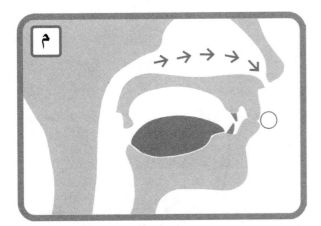

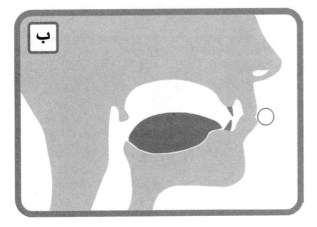

Wow

Wow is pronounced between the lips. The lips should be open, strongly contracted and protruding forwards leaving a small gap.

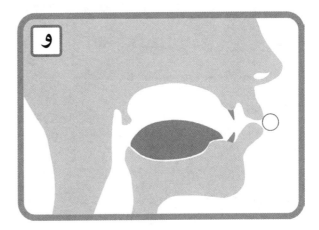

Faa

Faa is pronounced with the lower edges of the upper incisors touching the bottom inner part of the lip.

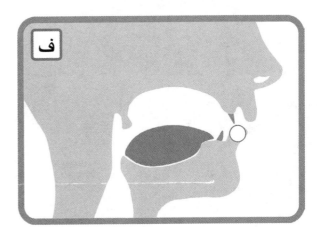

Tongue

There are eighteen letters that are pronounced with the tongue. There are two main sections of the tongue, tip and non tip.

Tip

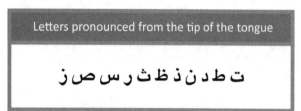

Letters pronounced from the tip of the tongue

ت ط د ن ذ ظ ث ر س ص ز

Taa, Daal and Tau

The tip of the tongue touches the root of the upper incisors and the first part of the roof of the mouth.

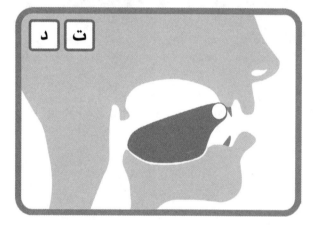

Tau

This is a heavy letter and the back of the tongue should be thick and elevated when pronouncing this letter.

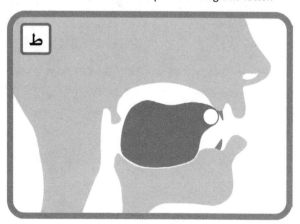

Noon

Noon is pronounced slightly further back. The tip and more of its surface touches the opposite part of the upper gum. The tongue does not touch the upper incisors. Noon is pronounced with Ghunna which is illustrated by the arrows on the diagram.

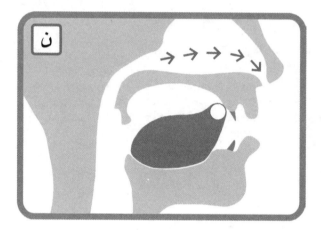

Raa

The larger part of the tip touches the opposite part of the inside upper gum. The tongue comes back down to the floor of the mouth, there is also a slight rolling sound. When Raa is pronounced with a heavy sound the tongue should be con-caved, thick and elevated. However Raa can be pronounced lightly, then the tongue should be relaxed on the floor of the mouth.

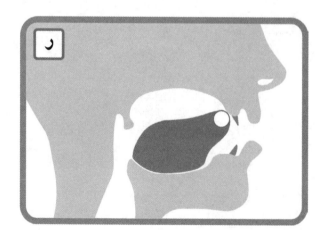

Thaa, Thaal and Thau

The tip of the tongue comes out slightly and touches the lower edges of the upper incisors.

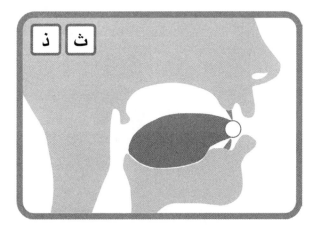

Zaa, Seen and Saud

The tip of the tongue touches the back of the lower incisors, with a small gap between the tip and the teeth.

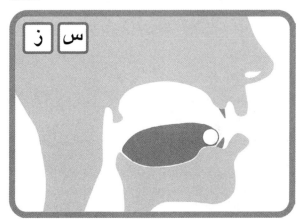

Thau

The tip of the tongue comes out slightly and touches the lower edges of the upper incisors. Thau is a heavy letter which is pronounced with a rounded sound with the tongue made thick and elevated at the back.

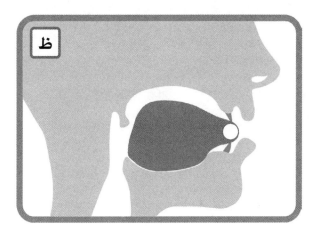

Saud

Saud is a heavy letters and is pronounced with a heavy sound with the tongue made thick and elevated.

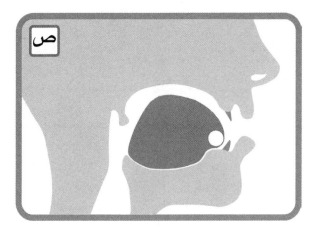

Non Tip

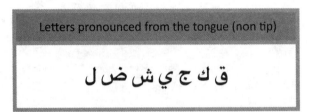

Letters pronounced from the tongue (non tip)

ق ك ج ي ش ض ل

Back of the Tongue
Qaaf and Kaaf

Qaaf is pronounced with the back part of the tongue touching the soft palate at the back of the mouth.

Kaaf is pronounced with the back part of the tongue touching the soft palate and the hard palate, but just before Qaaf.

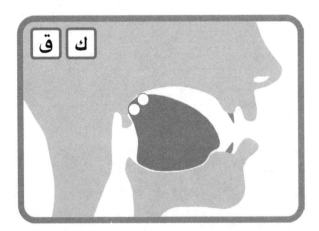

Middle of the Tongue

Jeem

The middle of the tongue touches the roof of the mouth.

Yaa and Sheen

Yaa and Sheen are also pronounced with the middle of the tongue touching the roof of the mouth but there is a slight gap between the tongue and the palate when pronouncing these letters.

Throat and Mouth Cavity (Jauf)

The letters pronounced from the open space in the mouth and throat cavity are known as Madd Tabee'ee which means Natural extension. These letters are:

Alif Madd - Fat-hah followed by Alif Saakin - extending the sound 'a' for 2 counts.

Yaa Madd - Kasrah followed by Yaa Saakin - extending the sound 'e' for 2 counts.

Wow Madd - Dammah followed by Wow Saakin - extending the sound 'u' for 2 counts.

The middle of the tongue is raised when pronouncing 'Yaa Madd' and the back part of the tongue is raised when pronouncing 'Wow Madd'. The tongue remains flat when pronouncing 'Alif Madd. This is shown in the following diagrams.

Side of the Tongue

Daud

When pronouncing this letter the sides (either one side or both side) of the tongue touches the upper molar teeth and pushes along the side of the teeth. This is a heavy letter with the tongue made thick and elevated.

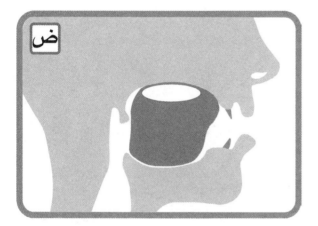

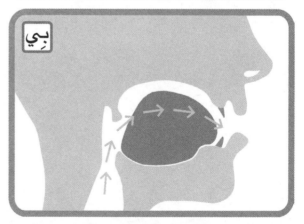

Laam

The tip and the front edges of the tongue touches the inside of the adjacent upper gum.

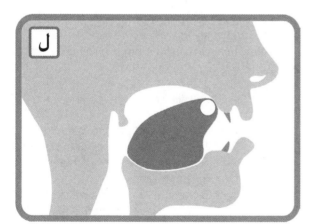

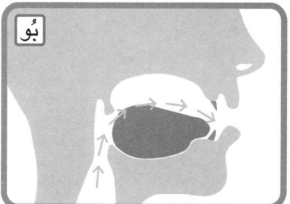

CHAPTER ONE
Makhaarij (Articulation point of each letter)
Recognition and Pronunciation of the Alphabet

LESSON 1
Letters Alif, Baa, Taa and Thaa

Teachers Top Tip

It is very important to tell the pupils the lesson objectives at the beginning of every lesson so they are clear about what they are going to learn. At the end of each lesson it is important to ask the pupils what they have learnt and if they feel they have achieved the objectives.

Objectives

To recognise the following letters:

Alif ا   **Baa** ب   **Taa** ت   **Thaa** ث

Pronunciation

The letter Alif is pronounced from the throat and mouth cavity and it never has a vowel. Alif is usually written with a Hamza on the top.

e.g. أ

It is the Hamza that is pronounced and not the Alif.

Hamza is pronounced from the bottom part of the throat.

Baa is pronounced between closed lips.

Taa is pronounced with the tip of the tongue touching the root of the upper incisors and the first part of the roof of the mouth.

Thaa the tip of the tongue comes out slightly and touches the lower edges of the upper incisors.

Teaching Steps

Explain the lesson objectives.

1. Using the website and the flashcards show the pupils the following letters:

ا   ب   ت   ث

Show the pupils how the letters can be written in different ways depending on if they are written at the beginning, middle or end of a word. Using the diagrams, on the reverse side of the flashcard, show the pupils where each letter is pronounced from and demonstrate how to say the letters.

Steps 2 to 5 are small activities for the children to complete.

2. Give the flashcards to the children, ask them to pronounce the letters and feel the shape of the letters at the same time, you can also ask the pupils to write the letters in the air with their fingers.

3. Ask the pupils to write the letters on a white board as many times as they want. You can make it more fun by writing big and small letters.

4. Ask the pupils to listen to the letters on the website (lesson 1.)

5. Ask the pupils to complete Section 1 in their book.

Conclude the lesson by asking the pupils what they have learnt.

Teaching Tip

Paint the letters you have learnt!

Objectives
To recognise the following letters:

Jeem ‎ج   Haa ‎ح   Khaa ‎خ

Pronunciation
Jeem the middle of the tongue touches the upper palate/roof.

Haa is pronounced from the middle of the throat.

Khaa is pronounced from the top part of the throat. It is a heavy letter so the sound is heavy and the back part of the tongue should be elevated.

Teaching Steps
Explain the lesson objectives.

1. Introduce the letters using the website and flashcards, demonstrate how to pronounce them. On the reverse side of the flash card show the pupils the diagrams to help them visualise where each letter comes from.
2. Give the flashcards to the pupils and ask them to pronounce the letters and feel the shape of the letters at the same time. Ask the pupils to write the letters in the air with their fingers.
3. Ask the pupils to write the letters on a white board.
4. Ask the pupils to listen to the letters on the website (lesson 2.)
5. Ask the pupils to complete Section 2 in their work book.

Conclude the lesson by asking the pupils what they have learnt.

Teaching Tip
Make the letters using play dough!

Objectives
To recognise the following letters:

Daal ‎د   Thaal ‎ذ

Pronunciation
Daal the tip of the tongue touches the roots of the front teeth and the roof of the mouth.

Thaal the tip of the tongue comes out slightly and touches the lower edges of the upper incisors.

Teaching Steps
Explain the lesson objectives.

1. Introduce the letters using the website and flashcards, demonstrate how to pronounce each letter. Show the pupils the diagrams to help them visualise where each letter comes from.
2. Ask the pupils to write the letters in the air.
3. Ask the pupils to write the letters on a white board.
4. Ask the pupils to listen to the letters on the website (Lesson 3.)
5. Ask the pupils to complete Section 3 in their work book.

Conclude the lesson by asking the pupils what they have learnt.

Teaching Tip
Make the letters out of pipe cleaners!

LESSON 4
Letters Raa and Zaa

LESSON 5
Letters Seen and Sheen

Objectives
To recognise the following letters:

Raa ر   Zaa ز

Objectives
To recognise the following letters:

Seen س   Sheen ش

Pronunciation
Raa the larger part of the tip (known as the dorsal) touches the inside upper gum then comes down again. When Raa is heavy, the tongue should be con-caved, thick and elevated.

Zaa the tip of the tongue touches the lower front teeth with a small gap between the tip and the teeth.

Pronunciation
Seen the tip of the tongue touches the back of the lower incisors, with a small gap between the tip and the teeth.

Sheen the middle of the tongue touches the upper palate/roof leaving a slight gap.

Teaching Steps
Explain the lesson objectives.

1. Introduce the letters using the website and flashcards, demonstrate how to pronounce them.
2. Give the flashcards to the pupils and ask them to pronounce the letters, feel the shape of the letters and write the letters in the air.
3. Ask the pupils to write the letters on the white board.
4. Ask the pupils to listen to the letters on the website (Lesson 4.)
5. Ask the pupils to complete Section 4 in their work book.

Conclude the lesson by asking the pupils what they have learnt.

Teaching Tip
Draw the letters in sand!

Teaching Steps
Explain the lesson objectives.

1. Introduce the letters using the website and flashcards, demonstrate how to pronounce them.
2. Ask the pupils to write the letters in the air.
3. Ask the pupils to write the letters on a white board.
4. Ask the pupils to listen to the letters on the website (Lesson 5.)
5. Ask the pupils to complete Section 5 in their work book.

Conclude the lesson by asking the pupils what they have learnt.

Teaching Tip
Draw the letters and colour them in!

Objectives
To recognise the following letters:

Saud ص   Daud ض

Pronunciation
Saud the tip of the tongue touches the back of the lower incisors, with a small gap between the tip and the teeth. It is a heavy letter, pronounced with a heavy sound and the tongue should be thick and elevated.

Daud the side (sides) of the tongue touches the upper back teeth and pushes close to the tip of the tongue. It is a heavy letter, pronounced with a heavy sound and the tongue should be thick and elevated.

Teaching Steps
Explain the lesson objectives.

1. Introduce the letters using the website and flashcards and demonstrate how to pronounce them.
2. Ask the pupils to write the letters in the air.
3. Ask the pupils to write the letters on the white board.
4. Ask the pupils to listen to the letters on the website (Lesson 6.)
5. Ask the pupils to complete Section 6 in their work book.

Conclude the lesson by asking the pupils what they have learnt.

Teaching Tip
Ask the pupils to draw and decorate their own letter cards for the letters they have learnt so far. These can also be used for a snap or pairs game!

Objectives
To recognise the following letters:

Tau ط   Thau ظ

Pronunciation
Tau the tip of the tongue touches the root of the front teeth and the roof of the mouth.

Thau the tip of the tongue comes out slightly and touches the lower edges of the upper incisors. Both of these letters are heavy and should be pronounced with a heavy sound and the tongue should be thick and raised.

Teaching Steps
Explain the lesson objectives.

1. Introduce the letters using the website and flashcards and demonstrate how to pronounce them.
2. Ask the pupils to write the letters in the air.
3. Ask the pupils to write the letters on a white board.
4. Ask the pupils to listen to the letters on the website (Lesson 7.)
5. Ask the pupils to complete Section 7 in their work book.

Conclude the lesson by asking the pupils what they have learnt.

Teaching Tip
See if you can find the letters you have learnt in the Quran!

Objectives
To recognise the following letters:

Ein ع   Ghayn غ

Pronunciation
Ein is pronounced from the middle of the throat.

Ghayn is pronounced from the top part of the throat, it is a heavy letter and the back part of the tongue should be elevated when pronouncing it.

Teaching Steps
Explain the lesson objectives.

1. Introduce the letters using the website and flashcards and demonstrate how to pronounce them.
2. Ask the pupils to write the letters in the air..
3. Ask the pupils to write the letters on a white board.
4. Ask the pupils to listen to the letters on the website (Lesson 8.)
5. Ask the pupils to complete Section 8 in their work book.

Conclude the lesson by asking the pupils what they have learnt.

Teaching Tip
Make the letters out of pasta shapes and stick them onto card!

Objectives
To recognise the following letters:

Faa ف   Qaaf ق   Kaaf ك

Pronunciation
Faa is pronounced with the lower edges of the upper incisors touching the bottom inner part of the lip.

Qaaf the very back part of the tongue is raised and it touches the soft palate at the back of the mouth. It is a heavy letter so a heavy sound should be pronounced.

Kaaf The back part of the tongue is raised and it is pronounced just before Qaaf. The back of the tongue touches the hard and soft palate at the back of the mouth.

Teaching Steps
Explain the lesson objectives.

1. Introduce the letters using the website and flashcards and demonstrate how to pronounce them.
2. Ask the pupils to write the letters in the air.
3. Ask the pupils to write the letters on a white board.
4. Ask the pupils to listen to the letters on the website (Lesson 9.)
5. Ask the pupils to complete Section 9 in their work book.

Conclude the lesson by asking the pupils what they have learnt.

Teaching Tip
Cut out the letters you have learnt.

LESSON 10
Letters Laam, Meem and Noon

LESSON 11
Letters Haa, Wow and Yaa

Objectives
To recognise the following letters:

Laam ل   Meem م   Noon ن

Objectives
To recognise the following letters:

Haa ـه   Wow و   Yaa ي

Pronunciation
Laam is pronounced with the front edges and the tip of the tongue touching the upper palate/roof of the mouth.

Meem is pronounced between closed lips (with Ghunna.)

Noon is pronounced with the tip of the tongue touching the inside upper gum, (with Ghunna.)

Pronunciation
Haa is pronounced from the bottom of the throat.

Wow is pronounced between the lips. The lips should be open, strongly contracted and protruding forwards leaving a small gap.

Yaa is pronounced with the middle of the tongue touching the middle part of the roof of the mouth leaving a slight gap.

Teaching Steps
Explain the lesson objectives.

1. Introduce the letters using the website and flashcards and demonstrate how to pronounce them.
2. Ask the pupils to write the letters in the air.
3. Ask the pupils to write the letters on a white board.
4. Ask the pupils to listen to the letters on the website (Lesson 10).
5. Ask the pupils to complete Section 10 in their work book.

Conclude the lesson by asking the pupils what they have learnt.

Teaching Steps
Explain the lesson objectives.

1. Introduce the letters using the website and flashcards and demonstrate how to pronounce them.
2. Ask the pupils to write the letters in the air.
3. Ask the pupils to write the letters on a white board.
4. Ask the pupils to listen to the website (Lesson 11.)
5. Ask the pupils to complete Section 11 in their work book.

Conclude the lesson by asking the pupils what they have learnt.

Teaching Tip
Colour the letters you have learnt!

Teaching Tip
Write the letter with glue on a piece of paper then sprinkle glitter on the glue. Shake off the excess glitter to make yourself a sparkly letter!

Objectives
To recognise and pronounce the letter Hamza.

Pronunciation
The letter Hamza can be written on its own and also on the letters Wow and Yaa. When Hamza is written on these letters it is always read as Hamza e.g.

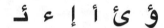

Hamza is pronounced from the bottom part of the throat.

Teaching Steps
Explain the lesson objectives.

1. Introduce the letters using the website and flashcards, demonstrate how to pronounce them.
2. Ask the pupils to write the letters in the air.
3. Ask the pupils to write the letters on a white board.
4. Ask the pupils to listen to the letters on the website (Lesson 12.)
5. Ask the pupils to complete Section 12 in their work book.

Conclude the lesson by asking the pupils what they have learnt.

Teaching Tip
Make an Arabic alphabet chart and stick it on the wall!

Objectives
To revise the letters of the alphabet

Teaching Steps
Explain the lesson objectives.

1. Using the flashcards ask the pupils to put the letters of the alphabet in the right order.
2. Ask the pupils to practice pronouncing each letter of the alphabet.
3. Ask the pupils to write all the letters on a white board.
4. Ask the pupils to listen to the letters on the website (Lesson 13).
5. Ask the pupils to complete Section 13 in their work book.

Conclude the lesson by asking the pupils what they have learnt.

Assessment sheets

In Book 1 of the Teacher's Guide there are Assessment
sheets at the end of each chapter. There is a sheet
for the pupils to read from, this sheet needs to be
photocopied for each child and given to them when
they are ready for the assessment. There is a teacher's
sheet for recording the pupil's progress. This sheet
has tick boxes for the teacher to record which letters
the pupil can read and a comment box at the bottom
of the sheet. This also needs to be photocopied for
each pupil and kept as a record for their progress.
The aim of the assessment is to inform the teachers
and parents of what the pupil has learnt so far and to
identify which areas need consolidating.

Name _____

أ	س	ت	ي	ل
ث	ن	ب	ش	ج
د	ظ	هـ	ع	خ
ح	ذ	ص	ر	ض
ط	ز	غ	ف	و
ق	ك	ل	م	ي

Name _____

أ ☐	س ☐	ت ☐	ي ☐	ل ☐
ث ☐	ن ☐	ب ☐	ش ☐	ج ☐
د ☐	ظ ☐	هـ ☐	ع ☐	خ ☐
ح ☐	ذ ☐	ص ☐	ر ☐	ض ☐
ط ☐	ز ☐	غ ☐	ف ☐	و ☐
ق ☐	ك ☐	ل ☐	م ☐	ي ☐

Objective	Comment Box

This chapter will teach children how to pronounce letters of the alphabet with:

- **Fat-hah**
- **Kasrah**
- **Dammah**

The Fat-hah, Kasrah and Dammah are sometimes known as short vowels or Harakah. They change how the letters are pronounced by adding a different sound.

- **Fat-hah** adds the sound **'a'**
- **Kasrah** adds the sound **'e'**
- **Dammah** adds the sound **'u'**

Each one is explained in further detail over the next three lessons. The lessons can be spaced out over a number of days.

Objectives
To read the letters of the alphabet with Fat-hah.

Recognition
A Fat-hah is a single slanted line that can be put on the top of any letter.

e.g.

Pronunciation
When a Fat-hah is written above a letter it is then pronounced with an 'a' sound like the 'a' found in the word 'cat'.
e.g.

Daal ﺩ with Fat-hah becomes Da

Jeem ﺝ with Fat-hah becomes Ja ﺝَ

Wow ﻭ with Fat-hah becomes Wa ﻭَ

Teaching Steps
Explain the lesson objectives.

1. Write some examples of letters with Fat-hah on the whiteboard and demonstrate how to pronounce each letter correctly.
2. Ask the pupils to write letters with a Fat-hah on a white board.
3. Ask the pupils to listen to the letters on the website (lesson 14.)
4. Ask the pupils to complete Section 14 in their work book.

Conclude the lesson by asking the pupils what they have learnt.

LESSON 15
Letters with Kasrah

LESSON 16
Letters with Dammah

Objectives
To read the letters of the alphabet with Kasrah.

Objectives
To read the letters of the alphabet with Dammah

Recognition
A Kasrah is a single slanted line that is written underneath any letter.

 e.g. رِ صِ

Recognition
A Dammah looks like a large coma or hook above the letter

 e.g. لُ بُ

Pronunciation
When a Kasrah is written beneath a letter it is pronounced with an 'e' sound like the 'e' found in the word he/she.
e.g.

Meem with a Kasrah becomes Me مِ

Taa with a Kasrah becomes Te تِ

Wow with a Kasrah becomes We وِ

Pronunciation
When a Dammah is written on top of a letter it is pronounced with an 'u' sound like the 'u' found in the word who or blue.
e.g.

Haa with Dammah becomes Hu حُ

Seen with Dammah becomes Su سُ

Kaaf with Dammah becomes Ku كُ

Teaching Steps
Explain the lesson objectives.

1. Write some examples of letters with Kasrah and demonstrate how to pronounce each letter correctly.
2. Ask the pupils to write the letters with a Kasrah on a white board.
3. Ask the pupils to listen to the letters on the website (Lesson 15.)
4. Ask the pupils to complete Section 15 in their work book.

Conclude the lesson by asking the pupils what they have learnt.

Teaching Steps
Explain the lesson objectives.

1. Write some examples of letters with Dammah on the whiteboard and demonstrate how to pronounce each letter correctly.
2. Ask the pupils to write the letters with a Dammah on a white board
3. Ask the pupils to listen to the letters on the website (lesson 16).
4. Ask the pupils to complete Section 16 in their work book.

Conclude the lesson by asking the pupils what they have learnt.

Teaching Tip
Make some letters with Fat-hah, Kasrah and Dammah out of playdough.

Name _____

جَ	لَ	سِ	حُ	ثَ
صُ	نَ	بُ	تِ	خِ
دُ	وَ	هِ	عُ	غِ
ضِ	شِ	مُ	زَ	رَ
ظِ	يَ	لُ	فِ	قَ
كِ	أَ	ذُ	طَ	ئَ

Name _____

جَ ☐	لَ ☐	سِ ☐	حُ ☐	ثَ ☐
صُ ☐	نَ ☐	بُ ☐	تِ ☐	خِ ☐
دُ ☐	وَ ☐	هِ ☐	عُ ☐	غِ ☐
ضِ ☐	شِ ☐	مُ ☐	زَ ☐	رَ ☐
ظِ ☐	يَ ☐	لُ ☐	فِ ☐	قَ ☐
كِ ☐	أَ ☐	ذُ ☐	طَ ☐	ىَ ☐

Objective	Comment Box

There are 3 lessons in this chapter.

Lesson 17 - Pronouncing letters with Sukoon.
Lesson 18 - Fat-hah followed by Wow Saakin
        (Leen letters.)
Lesson 19 - Fat-hah followed by Yaa Saakin
        (Leen letters.)

Objectives
To pronounce letters with Sukoon.

Recognition
A Sukoon is written above a letter and can be written either as a small triangular line or a small circle. It can be visible or invisible.

e.g. أَتْ

Pronunciation
Sukoon cannot be pronounced by itself, it will always have a letter with a vowel before it. A letter with Sukoon is pronounced as if the sound has stopped on the letter.
e.g.

لَمْ = Lam   أَتْ = At   قُلْ = Qul

Teaching Steps
Explain the lesson objectives.

1. Write some examples on a whiteboard of letters with Sukoon and demonstrate how to pronounce them correctly.
2. Ask the pupils to write some more examples on a white board.
3. Ask the pupils to listen to the letters with Sukoon on the website (Lesson 17.)
4. Ask the pupils to complete Section 17 in their work book.

Conclude the lesson by asking the pupils what they have learnt.

Teaching Tip
Draw some letters and words with sukoon in a sand tray.

LESSON 18
Leen Letters
(Letters with Fat-hah followed by Wow Saakin)

LESSON 19
Leen Letters
(Letters with Fat-hah followed by Yaa Saakin)

Objectives
To read and pronounce letters with Fat-hah followed by the letter Wow with Sukoon.

Objectives
To read and pronounce letters with a Fat-hah followed by a Yaa with Sukoon.

Pronunciation
A letter with Fat-hah which has a Wow Saakin after it is also called a Leen letter, it produces an 'ow' sound. Listen to the letters on the website before teaching them.
e.g.

نَوْ = Now   ثَوْ = Thow   سَوْ = Sow

Pronunciation
A letter with Fat-hah which has a Yaa Saakin after it is also called a Leen letter. It produces an 'ay' sound.
e.g.

بَيْ = Bay   تَيْ = Tay   كَيْ = Kay

Teaching Steps
Explain the lesson objectives.

1. Write some examples of letters on a whiteboard and demonstrate how to pronounce each letter correctly.
2. Ask the pupils to write some more examples on a white board.
3. Ask the pupils to listen to the letters on the website (Lesson 18.)
4. Ask the pupils to complete Section 18 in their work book.

Conclude the lesson by asking the pupils what they have learnt.

Teaching Tip
Look for some more examples in the Quran.

Teaching Steps
Explain the lesson objectives.

1. Write some examples on a whiteboard and demonstrate how to pronounce them correctly.
2. Ask the pupils to write some more examples on a white board.
3. Ask the pupils to listen to the letters on the website (Lesson 19).
4. Ask the pupils to complete Section 19 in the their work book.

Conclude the lesson by asking the pupils what they have learnt.

Teaching Tip
Make some more examples using pipe cleaners.

26

Name _____

أَتْ	لَمْ	أُسْ	أَخْ	ذَقْ
أَبْ	إِنْ	ثُبْ	أَجْ	سُكُ
حَيْ	بَيْ	تَيْ	نَيْ	وَيْ
طَيْ	ثَيْ	بَوْ	سَوْ	مَوْ
كَيْ	زَوْ	شَوْ	لَوْ	أَوْ

Name _____

أَتْ ☐	لَمْ ☐	أُسْ ☐	أَخْ ☐	ذَقْ ☐
أَبْ ☐	إِنْ ☐	ثُبْ ☐	أَجْ ☐	سُكْ ☐
حَيْ ☐	بِيْ ☐	تِيْ ☐	نِيْ ☐	وَيْ ☐
طَيْ ☐	ثِيْ ☐	بَوْ ☐	سَوْ ☐	مَوْ ☐
كَيْ ☐	زَوْ ☐	شَوْ ☐	لَوْ ☐	أَوْ ☐

Objective	Comment Box

CHAPTER FOUR
Madd Tabee'ee
(Natural Extension - Long vowels)

Introduction
This chapter will teach children how to recognise and pronounce the long vowels. The following extended sounds are called Madd Tabee'ee which is also known as natural Madd.

Recognition
The Madd letters that are taught in this chapter are:

Alif Madd - Fat-hah followed by Alif Saakin.
Yaa Madd - Kasrah followed by Yaa Saakin.
Wow Madd - Dammah followed by Wow Saakin.

These will be taught separately in the following lessons.

Pronunciation
The Madd letters are all pronounced from the empty space in the mouth and the top of the throat (Jauf.) The diagram below shows where the Madd sound is pronounced from.

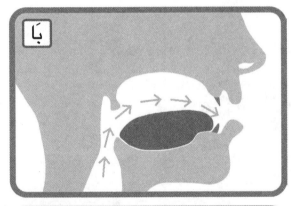

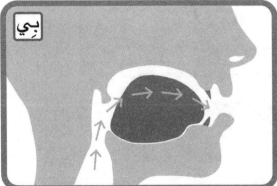

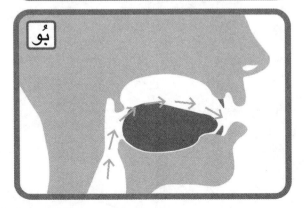

Objectives
- To recognise and pronounce Alif Madd correctly.
- To recognise the different ways the Alif Madd can be written in the Mus-haf.

Recognition
In the Mus-haf, the Alif can be written in the following ways.

1. Alif Saakin
When the letter is joined to the Alif.

e.g. بَا = 'Baa'   سَا = 'Saa'

2. Suspended Alif
The Alif can also be written in mid air.

e.g. تَ١ = ' Taa'   كَ١ = 'Kaa'

3. Long vowels with Alif Maqsurah
The Alif can be written as Alif Maqsurah (Yaa without dots). It can sometimes be written with a small Alif and sometimes empty. It can also be written on the letter Wow.

e.g. دَى = 'Daa'   لَى = 'Laa'

Pronunciation
The 'a' sound is extended for two counts. The sound of the Madd is pronounced from the empty space in the mouth and the top of the throat.

Teaching Steps
Explain the lesson objectives.
1. Show the pupils on the white board or website that when a letter with Fat-hah is followed by an Alif Saakin the sound is extended for two counts. Show the different ways the Alif can be represented.
2. Ask the pupils to write some examples of Alif Madd on a white board.
3. Ask the pupils to listen to the website (Lesson 20.)
4. Ask the pupils to complete Section 20 in their work book.

Conclude the lesson by asking the pupils what they have learnt.

Teaching Tip
Paint some letters with Alif Madd!

Objectives

To recognise and pronounce Yaa Madd correctly. (when a letter with Kasrah is followed by an empty Yaa, the vowel 'e' is held for two beats.)

Recognition

When a letter with Kasrah is followed by a Yaa with Sukoon. The Sukoon will not be visible and the Yaa can be written with or without the dots.

e.g.   بِى = 'Bee'   شِى = 'Shee'

e.g.   غِيضْ = ' Gheeda'   أَخِيه = 'Akheehe'

Pronunciation

This Madd is extended for two beats as 'ee'. It is pronounced from the empty space in the mouth and the top of the throat. (see earlier diagrams)

Teaching Steps

Explain the lesson objectives.

1. Show the pupils on the whiteboard that when a letter with Kasrah is followed by an Yaa Saakin the sound is extended for two counts.
2. Ask the pupils to write some examples of Yaa Madd on a white board.
3. Ask the pupils to listen to the letters on the website (Lesson 21.)
4. Ask the pupils to complete Section 21 in their work book.

Conclude the lesson by asking the pupils what they have learnt.

Teaching Tip

Look for some words with Yaa Madd in the Quran!

Objectives

To recognise and pronounce Wow Madd correctly. (when Dammah is followed by an empty Wow, the vowel 'u' is held for two beats).

Recognition

The Sukoon on the Wow will not be visible and the 'u' sound is lengthened up to 2 counts.

e.g.   نُو = 'Noo'   هُو = 'Hoo'

Pronunciation

The 'u' sound from the Dammah is extended for two beats as 'oo'. The sound of the Madd is pronounced from the empty space in the mouth and the top of the throat.

Teaching Steps

Explain the lesson objectives.

1. Show the pupils on the whiteboard that when a letter with Dammah is followed by an Wow Saakin the sound is extended for two counts.
2. Ask the pupils to write some examples of Wow Madd on a white board.
3. Ask the pupils to listen to the website (Lesson 22.)
4. Ask the pupils to complete Section 22 in their work book.

Conclude the lesson by asking the pupils what they have learnt.

Teaching Tip

Word hunt! Find some words with yaa madd in the Quran and practice reading them!

Name _____

شُو	مَىٰ	قَا	بِي	تَا
كَٰ	يُو	عَا	جُو	نَىٰ
حِي	وَٰ	ضَا	لَا	لِي
طَا	ثِي	كَا	بَىٰ	هُو
تَٰ	رَا	شِي	ظِي	دُو

Name _____

شُو ☐	مَىٰ ☐	قَا ☐	بِي ☐	تَا ☐
كَٰ ☐	يُو ☐	عَا ☐	جُو ☐	نَىٰ ☐
حِي ☐	وَٰ ☐	ضَا ☐	لَا ☐	لِي ☐
طَا ☐	ثِي ☐	كَا ☐	بَيْ ☐	هُو ☐
تَٰ ☐	رَا ☐	شِي ☐	ظِي ☐	دُو ☐

Objective	Comment Box

In this chapter the pupils will learn how to pronounce a letter with Tanween. The Tanween is an extra noon at the end of nouns, it involves adding a 'n' sound to the Fat-hah, Kasrah and dammah. There are three types of Tanweens:

Fat-hah Tanween - which makes 'an' sound, this is written on top of a letter. ⚍

Kasrah Tanween - which makes 'in' sound, this is written underneath a letter. ⚍

Dammah Tanween - which makes 'un' sound, this is written on top of a letter.

Each rule will be taught separately

Objectives
To recognise and pronounce the letters with Fat-hah Tanween.

Recognition
A Fat-hah Tanween is written as two Fat-hahs on top of each other e.g. Daal with a Tanween on the top looks like this ً (it is usually written with letter Alif after it which is ignored in continuation.)

Pronunciation

Daal ً with a Fat-hah Tanween is pronounced 'Dan'

Seen ً with a Fat-hah Tanween is pronounced 'San'

Teaching Steps
Explain the lesson objectives.

1. Write some examples on the whiteboard and demonstrate how to pronounce them correctly.
2. Ask the pupils to write some letters with Tanween on a white board.
3. Ask the pupils to listen to the sound of the letters on the website (Lesson 23.)
4. Ask the pupils to complete Section 23 in their work book.

Conclude the lesson by asking the pupils what they have learnt.

Teaching Tip
Make some letters with Tanween out of pipe cleaners!

LESSON 24
Letters with Kasrah Tanween

LESSON 25
Letters with Dammah Tanween

Objectives
To read the letters of the alphabet with Kasrah Tanween.

Objectives
To read the letters of the alphabet with Dammah Tanween

Recognition
A Kasrah Tanween is written as two Kasrahs on top of each other, it is written underneath the letters e.g. صٍ

Recognition
A Dammah Tanween can look like two Dammahs on top of each other or like a Dammah with a hook over the top.

e.g.   مٌ   مٌ

Pronunciation

Sheen with a kasrah Tanween شٍ it is pronounced as 'shin'.

Kaaf with a Kasrah Tanween كٍ it is pronounced as 'Kin'.

Pronunciation

Daal with a Dammah Tanween دٌ is pronounced as 'Dun'.

Taa with a Dammah Tanween تٌ is pronounced as 'Tun'.

Teaching Steps
Explain the lesson objectives.

1. Write some examples on the whiteboard and demonstrate how to pronounce them correctly.
2. Ask the pupils to write some letters with Tanween on a white board.
3. Ask the pupils to listen to the sound of the letters on the website (Lesson 24.)
4. Ask the pupils to complete Section 24 in their work book.

Conclude the lesson by asking the pupils what they have learnt.

Teaching Steps
Explain the lesson objectives.

1. Write some example on the whiteboard and demonstrate how to pronounce them correctly.
3. Ask the pupils to write some letters with Tanween on a white board.
4. Ask the pupils to listen to the sound of the letters on the website (Lesson 25.)
5. Ask the pupils to complete Section 25 in their work book.

Conclude the lesson by asking the pupils what they have learnt.

Teaching Tip
Make some letters with Tanween using play-dough.

Teaching Tip
Make your own flashcards for letters with Tanween.

Name _____

بَا	طُوْ	سٍ	گَا	تُوْ
عَا	ثٍ	مُوْ	يَا	أَ
رَا	شُوْ	ضٍ	صُّ	خَّ
فِ	هُوْ	كِ	قَّا	نِ
دُوْ	زَّا	قُوْ	نِ	وِ

Name _____

تُۢ ☐	گَّا ☐	سٍ ☐	طُۢ ☐	بَّا ☐
أَ ☐	يَّا ☐	مُۢ ☐	ثٍ ☐	عَّا ☐
خَّا ☐	صُۢ ☐	ضٍ ☐	شُۢ ☐	رَّا ☐
نٍ ☐	قَّا ☐	كٍ ☐	هُۢ ☐	فٍ ☐
وِ ☐	نِ ☐	قُۢ ☐	زَّا ☐	دُۢ ☐

Objective	Comment Box

In this chapter the children will be taught how to recognise and pronounce the letters of the alphabet with Shaddah.

Recognition

A Shaddah is always written above a letter e.g. بّ

Pronunciation

A Shaddah represents a double letter, the letter before is joined to the letter with Shaddah.

e.g. رَبّ is pronounced as Rabba with a stress on the Baa.

Objectives

To read letters with Shaddah.

Teaching Steps

Explain the lesson objectives.

1. Write some examples on a whiteboard and demonstrate how to pronounce them.
2. Ask the pupils to write some letters with Shaddah on a white board.
3. Ask the pupils to listen to the sound of a letter with Shaddah on the website (Lesson 26.)
4. Ask the pupils to complete Section 26 in their work book.

Conclude the lesson by asking the pupils what they have learnt.

Name _____

أَيَّ	جَنَّ	مَدَّ	تَبَّ	أَنَّ
شَرِّ	صَبَّ	قَلَّ	ظَنَّ	صَلِّ
مِلَّةَ	كُلِّ	مِمَّ	ظِلِّ	رَبَّ
قَدَّ	إِنَّ	إِلَّا	عَلَّمَ	قُوَّةَ

Name _____

أَنَّ	تَبَّ	مَدَّ	جَنَّ	أَيَّ
صَلِّ	ظَنَّ	قَلَّ	صَبَّ	شَرِّ
رَبَّ	ظَلِّ	مِمَّ	كُلِّ	مَلَّةَ
قُوَّةً	عَلَّمَ	إِلَّا	إِنَّ	قَدَّ

Objective	Comment Box

Date _____

Objectives

Introduction

Activities

Evaluation

Tajweed - To improve, make better. The correct pronunciation during recitation & following the rules of tajweed.

Makhaarij - The point of articulation of a letters, or the point at which the sound stops.

Fat-hah - Is a type of short vowel. It is always written above the letter. The way of pronunciation is by separating the jaws and opening the mouth to make the sound 'a'.

Kasrah - Is a type of short vowel. It is always below the letter. The way of pronunciation is by dropping the lower jaw to make the sound 'e'.

Dammah - Is a type of short vowel. It is always above the letter and looks like an apostrophe.. The way of pronunciation is by rounding and protruding the two lips the make the sound 'u'.

Ghunna - The sound that is produced from the nasal cavity.

Tanween - It is a hidden noon Saakin that occurs at the end of nouns. It is a vowel that produces a "n" sound immediately after it.

Shaddah - The doubling of sound.

Sukoon - A small semi or full circle written above a letter. This represents a letter which does not have a vowel. It also joins two letters.

After completing this book the pupils should now be secure with all of the rules that have been covered from the Makharaj of each letter, to pronouncing letters with Shaddah. Keep practising and listening to the pupils recite the Quran to ensure they are confident with what they have learnt. Revisit any rules that need consolidating and if necessary repeat some of the work sheets.

Once the pupils are confident with the rules taught in this book move on to Book 2. When the pupils have completed both books they will have covered enough Tajweed rules to be able to recite fluently.